The Loves of Cass McGuire

BY BRIAN FRIEL

PLAYS
Philadelphia, Here I Come!
The Loves of Cass McGuire

STORIES
The Saucer of Larks
The Gold in the Sea

The Loves of Cass McGuire

A PLAY BY BRIAN FRIEL

FARRAR
STRAUS
AND
GIROUX
New York

Published simultaneously in Canada by Ambassador Books, Ltd.,
Rexdale, Ontario

Printed in the United States of America

Library of Congress catalog card number: 67-11943

Designed by Betty Crumley

Grateful acknowledgment is made to the following for permission
to reprint copyrighted material: To Hugh Noyes and to J. B. Lippincott
Company for permission to quote from "The Highwayman" by
Alfred Noyes, from Collected Poems in One Volume, copyright 1906,
1934 by Alfred Noyes. To The Macmillan Company, A. P. Watt & Son,
The Macmillan Company of Canada and M. B. Yeats, for permission
to quote from "He Wishes for the Cloths of Heaven," by William
Butler Yeats, from The Collected Poems, copyright 1906 by The
Macmillan Company, renewed 1934 by William B. Yeats.

For Nano and Mary

Note

In my description of the set I mention that the winged chair is never used throughout the play except during the three rhapsodies. These occur, one in each act, as part of the formal pattern or ritual of the action; and the musical term "rhapsody" seemed to me to be the most accurate description of them. Each of the three characters who rhapsodize—Trilbe, Ingram, and Cass—takes the shabby and unpromising threads of his past life and weaves them into a hymn of joy, a gay and rapturous and exaggerated celebration of a beauty that might have been. (To pursue the musical imagery a stage further, and as a signpost for future productions, I consider the play to be a concerto in which Cass McGuire is the soloist.)

When I wrote the play, I envisaged these rhapsodies being played against a musical background; and I chose Wagner because his *Tristan und Isolde* legend has parallels of sorts in Cass McGuire's story. But during rehearsals I discovered that two of the actors spoke their rhapsodies with such grace and dignity, invested their soliloquies with such cantabile magic, that any background music would have been a distraction. So Wagner was dropped. But I have left the directions for the music in the text because subsequent companies may not be so fortunate in their rhapsodists and they may be grateful for the potent crutch that the "Liebestod," for example, affords.

BRIAN FRIEL

Derry City
North Ireland
October 1966

Cast

HARRY MCGUIRE

DOM MCGUIRE, *Harry McGuire's youngest son*

MOTHER, *his mother*

ALICE, *his wife*

CASS, *his sister*

TESSA, *maid in Eden House*

PAT QUINN

TRILBE COSTELLO

MR. INGRAM

MRS. BUTCHER

All residents in Eden House

Set

A spacious, high-ceilinged room, somewhere between elegance and austerity, which serves as the common room in Eden House, a home for old people, and also as the living room in the home of Harry McGuire, a wealthy Irish businessman-accountant.

The back wall consists of glass and French windows which open out to a formal garden where a Cupid statue (illuminated) is frozen in an absurd and impossible contortion.

A large marble fireplace on wall right (from the point of view of the audience). Round mahogany table center stage. Two fireside chairs and several upright chairs.

Downstage right, conspicuous in its isolation, is a big winged armchair. This is never used throughout the play except during the three rhapsodies.

Upstage left, on a raised platform, is a bed, a bedside table, and a chair. This area will be Cass's bedroom in Eden House. It will be black when the curtain first rises.

TIME: *The present in Ireland*

ACT I: *Two weeks before Christmas. Morning*
ACT II: *One week before Christmas. Afternoon*
ACT III: *Christmas Eve. Evening*

ACT ONE

When the curtain rises, GRAN MCGUIRE, HARRY'S *mother, is sitting in her wheelchair, and young* DOM *is huddled over the fire, reading a True Detective comic.* GRAN *is eighty-nine and almost totally deaf. Black satin blouse, a rug around her knees, and a black shawl which has fallen from her shoulders. Were she able to walk around, she would have the authority and self-possession of a queen; but because she is invalided, she just looks monumental. The serene, superior expression on her face never varies because nothing can touch her now. Her speech is slow and dignified.*

DOM, *aged seventeen, wears flannels and a school blazer. He is too big physically to be a schoolboy and not yet a young man, and is conscious of his gaucheness.*

He looks furtively at the door, takes a cigarette from his pocket, lights it, and inhales ostentatiously. Then goes on reading.

MOTHER

The next question is an easy one. Hands up any child who can tell me the name of the new cardinal. Anyone in the class know?

DOM

Captain Mike O'Shea, Vice-Squad Headquarters, Forty-seventh Precinct.

MOTHER

I beg your pardon?

DOM

"O'Shea flung his men around the building and dashed inside. The startled Samoan girls in varying forms of undress ran screaming into Madam Lulana's room." Wow-wow-wow-wow!

MOTHER

I'm afraid you'll have to raise your voice a little.

DOM

You're a deaf and doting old bag of guts. D'you know why Madam Lulana kept only Samoan girls? Because all they think of is sex, Gran—just like you and me. And no matter what climate they're in, they never wear underclothes.

MOTHER

And I'm told that Cardinal Logue is a brilliant classical scholar, too.

DOM

I'll tell you a secret, Gran: when I leave school, I'm going to set up a business of my own, right here in town—a kip house. And I'll make you the madam. And anyone that tries to get too smart, you'll give them the old knee in the groin—one-two-three—Gorgeous Gran McGuire, the Sailors' Terror!

MOTHER

I want everyone to repeat that ten times.

DOM

Gorgeous Gran McGuire, the Sailors' Terror; Gorgeous Gran McGuire, the Sailors' Terror; Gorgeous Gran McGuire, the Sailors' . . .

He breaks off when he hears his mother approach left. Throws the cigarette into the fire after a desperate effort to nick it and dashes back to the table, where his schoolbooks are impressively arrayed. Sticks the True Detective into his jacket pocket. He is studying when his mother enters.

ALICE *is in her fifties. She is expensively, but not attractively, dressed. She notices* DOM's *scramble to get a schoolbook opened. She is carrying chairbacks for the fireside chairs.*

ALICE

I thought you were studying.

DOM

Gran and I were discussing the hierarchy.

ALICE

I hear your father's car. Put your books away and take

your grandmother with you into the dining room.

DOM

Lunch ready?

ALICE

Yours is. We aren't eating until later.

DOM

What about Auntie Cass?

ALICE

Still asleep.

DOM

Can I bring up her tray?

ALICE

No.

DOM

I've bought a bar of chocolate for her.

ALICE

I said she's asleep.

DOM

No wonder. I could hear her singing at the top of her voice
half the night.

ALICE

That'll do, Dom.

DOM

She must be feeling terrible today. Just as well Madam Gran is deaf. (*Articulating into* GRAN'*s ear*) She called you, her own mother, a big cow!

ALICE

Dom, please!

MOTHER

You'll not forget this day.

DOM

(*solemnly*): It's engraved on our hearts in letters of gold.

Enter HARRY *left. Good black coat, soft hat, carrying a paper. He is sixty but looks younger. A measured, middle-of-the-road man, well in control of himself. He has his mother's soft, attractive voice. He gives* ALICE *a perfunctory kiss, hands her the coat and hat, and sits at the fire.*

ALICE

You're late, aren't you?

HARRY

I had a few calls to make. How are you today, Mother? Dom.

ALICE
Will you have a drink?

HARRY
Brandy, please. And nothing in it.

ALICE
You and I are having a light lunch.

HARRY
?

ALICE
The Traynors are coming to dinner tonight.

HARRY
Hell.

ALICE
(*leaving*): They're your friends.

HARRY
How's the work going?

DOM
All right.

HARRY
I phoned the college and told them you had a cold.

(*Pause*) How is it?

DOM

All right.

HARRY

You're sure you don't want a grind during the Christmas holidays?

DOM

No . . . no . . .

HARRY

I can get young Coyle to come to the house, you know.

DOM

No, it's . . . all right.

HARRY

A matter for yourself. (*Nods and smiles at* GRAN) Mother.

MOTHER

They tell me the beaches are crowded.

HARRY

It's freezing outside.

MOTHER

I'm thinking seriously of investing in a parasol.

ALICE *enters with a drink and a letter. She hands both to Harry.*

ALICE
A letter from Betty. They bought that house after all.

HARRY
How much?

ALICE
Seventeen thousand.

HARRY
Very nice.

ALICE
And they're coming for Christmas—with the baby.

HARRY
That's good news. We'll have a full house. (*Opening letter*) Mother seems to think it's summer.

ALICE
She has been teaching me Latin roots all morning. Anything fresh downtown?

HARRY
Not a thing. Here?

ALICE
All quiet so far.

HARRY

She hasn't appeared yet?

ALICE

Not a sound. Did you find out where she was? What happened?

HARRY

Where was she not. I called in Sweeny's pub on the way home and paid for the breakages. Apparently every table in the lounge was an antique.

ALICE

And the police?

HARRY

The sergeant was with me. I squared that. Dom!

ALICE

And the clay on her shoes—how did she get it?

HARRY

Bring my briefcase in from the car, son, please.

ALICE

You've got to do something, Harry.

The subdued domestic atmosphere is suddenly and violently shattered by CASS's *shouts. She charges on stage (either from the wings or from the auditorium), shouting in her raucous Irish-American voice. Everyone on stage freezes.*

CASS *is a tall, bulky woman of seventy. She wears a gaudy jacket (because of the cold weather) over gaudy clothes; rings, earrings; two voluminous handbags which never leave her. She smokes incessantly and talks loudly and coarsely (deliberately at times). Ugly is too strong a word to describe her, and plain not nearly strong enough. If she ever had good features once, there is no trace of them now. A life of hard physical work has ravaged her. Only her spirit is strong and resilient.*

CASS

What the hell goes on here?

ALICE

Cass!

HARRY

Cass, you can't break in, Cass, at—!

CASS *addresses the audience direct. They are her friends, her intimates. The other people on stage are interlopers.*

CASS

Cass! Cass! Cass! I go to the ur-eye-nal for five minutes and they try to pull a quick one on me!

HARRY

The story has begun, Cass.

CASS

The story begins where I say it begins, and I say it begins with me stuck in the gawddam workhouse! So you can all get the hell outa here!

HARRY

The story begins in the living room of my home, a week after your return to Ireland. This is my living room and we're going to show bit by bit how you came—

CASS

(*looking around set*): Sure! Real nice and cozy! (*Direct to audience*) The home of my brother, Mister Harold McGuire, accountant, brick manufacturer, big-deal Irish businessman. Married to Alice, only child of Joe Connor, the lawyer, who couldn't keep his hands off young girls.

HARRY

That's enough, Cass!

CASS

Four kids: one a lady doctor; one an architect; one a clergyman; and one a student—if I may say so. What else do they (*audience*) need to know?

ALICE

Harry, for heaven's sake!

CASS

(*looking around*): Yeah, this'll do for the workhouse. We have swank windows, too, opening out onto a garden, only we don't have a nekked kid holding his hands in front of his rice crispies all day.

HARRY

This isn't fair to us, Cass. It must be shown slowly and in sequence why you went to Eden House.

CASS

I didn't go, Harry boy, I was stuck in! Oh, sure, sure, go back and show them how patient you all were with the terrible woman that appeared out of the blue after fifty-two years! How her momma doesn't reconnize her, and how her brother is embarrassed by her, and how Alice—Jeez, yes—I think poor Alice is afraid of her! You afraid of me, Alice?

ALICE

Harry—!

HARRY

Cass, I insist we unfold the story in proper sequence!

CASS

And then this day she goes and visits her father's grave— that's how she got the clay on her shoes, sweetie—and then gets plastered and kicks up a bit of a shindy in a downtown

bar, and someone calls the cops, and someone keeps screaming, "It's Mr. McGuire's sister, the returned Yankee!" and
then her folks have this big solemn meeting—I just saved
you all that—and decide to stick her into the workhouse
and—

HARRY

Eden House is a rest home for elderly people.

CASS

Listen to him! He could sell fur coats to chow dawgs in the
Sahara. So we're going to skip all that early stuff, all the
explanations, all the excuses, and we'll start off later in
the story—from here (*light up bed area*). My suite in the
workhouse, folks. Drop in and see me some time, okay?
Where the hell was I? (*Remembering*) Yeah—the home-
coming—back to the little green isle. Well, that's all over
and done with—history; and in my book yesterday's dead
and gone and forgotten. So let's pick it up from there, with
me in the—rest home. (*To* HARRY, *who is about to go off
stage*) Go ahead and call out the National Guard if you
like; but you're not going to move me! What's this god-
dam play called? The Loves of Cass McGuire. Who's Cass
McGuire? Me! Me! And they'll see what happens in the
order *I* want them to see it; and there will be no going
back into the past!

MOTHER

The present Chief Justice is a past pupil of mine.

CASS

And I'm Garibaldi's mistress. And this ain't no visiting day
in Eden House. So get the hell outa here, all of you. Go on,
go on; clear. You too, professor (DOM). The less you see of
your old Auntie Cass the better, because she ain't got no
money, and we suspect she doesn't go to church, and we're
not too sure if she's a maiden aunt at all.

ALICE *quickly signals to her family to leave.*

HARRY

You'll regret this, Cass.

CASS

I regret nuthin'.

HARRY

You may think you can seal off your mind like this, but
you can't. The past will keep coming back to you.

CASS

I live in the present, Harry boy! Right here and now!

HARRY

We have a point of view, too, and in fairness to all of us—

*At the word "fairness" she makes an extravagant dismissing ges-
ture with her hand.*

CASS

Aaaaaaaaagh!

She moves into her bedroom and sits on the bed. HARRY *holds a brief consultation with his family, and apparently they decide to go away because they move off. Now that she is alone with the audience, her friends,* CASS *is much more subdued. She talks to them almost confidentially. But the past scene has disturbed her more than she would like to admit: her hands are shaking. She fumbles for a cigarette and lights it. Then she makes up. During all this business she addresses the audience.*

CASS

Well, that stirred things up a bit, dinnit? The past—poof! (*To herself in hand mirror*) Ugh! It's not like whisky, beautiful; the years don't improve it. (*Remembering*) Like there was this bum used to come in for breakfast every morning into this joint on the lower East Side I worked in. Boy, you should ov seen his hands! Joe Bolowski, that was his name; they said he was a concert pianist or something before he messed hisself up. Anyways, Joe would look at me like I was the blazing July sun or something, and he would say, "Honey, I pulled the chain on better-looking things." Asked me to marry him, too. Every Friday night. When he was drunk. (*Producing half bottle of whisky from one of the bags*) Helluva guy, Joe. (*Drinks straight from bottle*) To the future . . . Shhhh.

INGRAM *appears outside French windows. After a few seconds, he is joined by* COSTELLO.

CASS

See that? That's old Ingram. She's probably there with
him—Trilbe Costello. Trilbe—now there's a name for you!
I sez to her the first day, "You some kind of hat or something?" They're gooks, okay, real gooks, phew . . . He
played the organ in some swank English cathedral, he
tells me; and she was—you know—a professor of speech
and elocution and all that crap. Real swank. Always talking about poetry and music and stuff. And as Pat Quinn
sez—you'll see him around, too; a good guy, Pat—as he
sez, you'd think they'd be past all that now, wouldn't you?
Kinda sweet, though, aren't they? And there's something
about old Ingram, I dunno, maybe it's the quiet way he
talks, but he reminds me of Harry.

In the gloom immediately beyond CASS's *bed,* HARRY *appears in
his dressing gown and slippers. He talks softly, gently, and* CASS
*answers him in a remote tone at first. He looks at her, but she
stares straight down into the auditorium. This is the first of the
memory sequences that haunt* CASS. *Some of them she keeps at
bay by talking resolutely to the audience. But some are so potent
that she is seduced into reliving them.*

HARRY

You should have let me run you out in the car, Cass.

CASS

I wanted to be alone.

HARRY

The grave's nice. And the flowers. Alice planted them.

CASS

Pretty flowers.

HARRY

We got a stone mason up from Cork to do the headstone.

CASS

I sent ten dollars. All I had at the time.

HARRY

Apparently Father had been living for over twenty years in a—sort of doss house, right in the center of Glasgow. They lived in a two-roomed flat on the ground floor.

CASS

Three weeks buried before I even knew.

HARRY

He must have told this woman he was a widower because she asked me how long Mother was dead. I didn't—tell Alice that.

CASS

(*briskly to audience*): There was this guy owned the joint I worked in . . .

HARRY

He looked much older than seventy-six. The woman said he had been invalided for the last five years.

CASS

—I told you about it—a breakfast counter . . .

HARRY

Oh, yes, I forgot: she said Father talked a lot about his daughter Cass.

CASS

Jeff Olsen was his name. And he had this dawg, see, this bitch, and we lived in this two-roomed apartment . . .

HARRY

What age were you when he went away, Cass? Fifteen? Sixteen?

CASS

—and when that bitch would get high, she would yap-yap-yap, and all the dawgs in the block they would yap-yap-yap back—O Jeez—until everyone was screaming murder.

HARRY

I was only five when he left. I have no memory of him at all.

CASS

So, Jeff, first he got that bitch desexed; and then when that done no good he got it debarked—you know, so that it couldn't bark no more; and there was this bum, Slinger, from down South, sometimes he took coffee in our joint, and when Jeff told him about the dawg being desexed and debarked, Slinger said, "Nothin' left for it but to dee-cease, Jeff." Real funny guy, you know . . .

HARRY

She knew all about his job on the old railway, and how you would hide in the signal box with him when you should have been at school with Mother.

CASS

(*brutally*): That's finished! All over!

HARRY *drifts into the darkness of the wings.*

CASS

And I don't go in for the fond-memory racket! For fifty-two years I work one block away from Skid Row—dead-beats, drags, washouts, living in the past! Washing, scrubbing, fixing sandwiches—work so that you don't have no time to think, and if you did you thought of the future. (*Fumbling greedily for the bottle*) The past's gone. Good luck to it. And Gawd bless it. (*Drinks. Then lights another cigarette*)

TESSA, *the maid, enters from the right. She is distributing clean pillowcases for the beds. The boredom and drudgery of working with old people have made her weary at eighteen. She is untidy in appearance (until Act Three) and protects herself from the senility around her by an acquired casualness of manner. When she sees her,* CASS *hides the bottle.*

TESSA

You're almost a week in the house now and you know fine well you're not allowed in your bedroom between breakfast and teatime.

CASS

Sweet little Tessa.

TESSA

And another thing: unless you're sick, you're supposed to be down in the oratory for Mass in the morning.

CASS

What time's that at?

TESSA

Seven.

CASS

I'm always in the d.t.'s till ten at least.

TESSA

Will you move? How can I fix the bed with you on it?

CASS

You've got a point there.

While TESSA *changes the pillowcase,* CASS *gathers her things to go to the common room.*

TESSA

Are you a bed wetter?

CASS

Only when I'm waiting to be raped, sweetie.

TESSA *goes off left.* CASS *goes upstage. At the same time,* PAT QUINN *enters right. A small, plump man, assured, confident, cunning, the know-all of the institution. Anxious to please. In his early sixties.*

CASS

Hi, Pat.

PAT

How are you, Miss McGuire?

CASS

Where is everybody?

PAT

All in bed, pretending they're sick, on account of the cold weather.

CASS

Ain't they got no peat around here now?

PAT

The boiler's busted. But by the time they get around to fixing it, I'll be gone—back to the nephew's farm.

CASS

(*not listening, searching bag*): You bet.

PAT

He has five hundred acres and three hundred and fifty head of cattle. I'm only temporary here, you know, until himself and the missus move into the new house.

CASS

Same here. I'm temporary, too.

PAT

He's chairman of the Young Farmers League.

CASS

Big deal.

PAT

And I keep an eye on the men when he's away at the meetings.

CASS

You going downtown today, Pat?

PAT

I'm on my way out now for the papers.

CASS

You know that store right next the post office?

PAT

What place is that now?

CASS

The first store below the post office on the same side.

PAT

Is it Sweeny's pub you're talking about?

CASS

You go in there and ask the bartender—Tommy's his name—you ask him for the same again for Miss McGuire.

PAT

The same again . . . ?

CASS

And have one on me outa the change.

PAT

Is it . . . drink . . . for you?

CASS

It's not baby powder I'm looking for!

PAT

Holy God, if the matron caught me at that game!

CASS

(*taking back money*): Gimme. Someone else'll get it for me.

PAT

No, no, it's all right. A wee drop now and again is good for the health.

CASS

That's it, Pat. Look at the woman it made of me.

TRILBE COSTELLO *bursts in, followed by* MR. INGRAM. *She is in her early seventies but is full of energy. She has been an elocution teacher all her life—but without the necessary qualifications and consequently never recognized by the education department—and her speech and manner both reflect this: she articulates fanatically and is inclined to domineer. At the same time one is conscious of an insecurity behind the extravagant exterior.*

MR. INGRAM *is a small, withered, testy, nervous old man. He is English. He is so frail and hesitant that he seldom finishes a sentence. He carries large volumes with him everywhere he goes. Now, as they enter,* TRILBE *is consulting some sheets of paper and at the same time addressing an imaginary group of people.* CASS *is still new to* TRILBE *and views her with open wonder.* PAT *knows* TRILBE *well and humors her.*

TRILBE

Before I announce the results of the competition I would like to take this opportunity to thank all those young boys and girls who came up here so bravely and spoke their test piece with such courage and gusto. A very sincere thank you to you, indeed.

PAT

There you are, now.

CASS

Hi.

TRILBE

(*softly*): Morning. Morning. I'm adjudicating at a speech festival for junior schools next week. Just a little rehearsal.

CASS

Sure, sure—you just blast ahead.

TRILBE

You know "The Highwayman," don't you?

CASS

Which one? Where I worked, they were all—

TRILBE

"The wind was a torrent of darkness among the gusty
   trees,

*The moon was a ghostly galleon tossed upon cloudy
seas . . ."*

PAT

There's speaking for you!

TRILBE

Noyes.

CASS

Well, maybe just a little—

TRILBE

Alfred J. Noyes. Not his best, but it fires the young imag-
ination. Next Thursday. You're welcome if you choose to
come. (*Adjudicating again and moving slowly off*) I liked
in particular competitors number 7, 8, and 13, whose sense
of rhythm really stirred me. *"Tlot-tlot in the empty silence,
tlot-tlot in the echoing night."* Thrilling.

INGRAM

It is our experience . . . we find . . . we find that one
doesn't feel the cold so . . . so . . . if one keeps on the
move and doesn't . . .

TRILBE

Mr. Ingram!

INGRAM

Coming, Miss Costello. We walk round past the refectory

and along the . . . it's a very pleasant little . . . good
morning . . .

CASS *looks after them as they exit right.*

CASS

Boy, would Ed Sullivan eat them up!

PAT

Adjudicating! That one—sure she wasn't even qualified
to teach that elocution stuff! Running about the country-
side from the nuns to the brothers, scrounging meals and
picking up an odd shilling here and there. A tramp with
notions—that's what that one is!

CASS

(*mopping her face*):   Can she spit!

PAT

The Costellos from Ardbeg—didn't I know them all in my
day. All highfalutin chat and not a penny to scratch them-
selves with. Your mother there could tell you all about
them.

CASS

I'm sure *she* could. You going downtown, Pat, or are you
not?

PAT

(*leaving*):   I'll be back in ten minutes. The same again

for Miss McGuire. And no one'll know a word about it. By the way, boiled bacon for dinner, and stewed apples after.

Exits

CASS *sits down in the common room, lights a cigarette, and addresses the audience.*

CASS

Wonderful! And prunes for breakfast. All I need now is to go on a rum bash. Funny title, too, innit? The Loves of Cass McGuire—like I was Mata Hari or something. I'm seventy, by the way. And Harry, he's pushing sixty. And Momma she's . . . gee, Momma must be eighty-nine now . . . yeah . . . cos Father he was three years older than her. He sailed off when I was a kid—just to fill you in on the background—cos Momma and him didn't hit it off too well when he took a drop. Never wrote nor nothing. Just got hisself lost in Scotland. So, when I was eighteen, I kinda got the same idea, you know; not that Momma and me didn't hit it off; we got on okay, I guess, but . . . Well, what the hell was there to do around here, I mean? Oh boy, she raised Cain, I'll tell you; real schoolteacher stuff; sent for Father O'Neill to speak to me and all . . . (*Remembering*) Now, whatever happened to him? Dead, I guess. He was some guy, you know: big and heavy and this voice like a foghorn. Should ov been in the Marines.

(*Laughs gently*) The night he caught Connie Crowley guzzling the hell outa me below the crooked bridge! "You bastard," he sez—well, mebbe he didn't use that word— "Are you comfortable in your sinning?" And poor Connie, Jeez I could feel his knees going, he sez, "Please, no, Father. The grass's damp." Anyways, I saved up and gathered the passage money and left a note for Momma and one for Connie . . . and off I blew . . . (*looks around the room*) and back I come home to my own people—and they have this big solemn meeting—and decide to kick me out!

HARRY *strides on from right, his coat across his arm. He is very stern but tries to control himself. She is aware of what he is saying to her but talks on resolutely to the audience.*

HARRY

I've just been told what happened this morning, Cass.

CASS

So now you know it all.

HARRY

And I will not have you insult Alice about her father.

CASS

Harry's four kids, boy, they got on good: Betty she's a doc in London, and Tom's a priest, and Aiden's an architect, and Dom—

HARRY

But this is only the last of many, many insults.

CASS

Fine kids—I haven't met them yet—but you'll see, they'll be along one of these days to meet their Auntie Cass—

HARRY

And before I say any more I want you to know that the decision I've made is entirely my own. Alice had nothing to do with it.

CASS

Betty she has a baby—fourteen months—I seen pictures of it.

HARRY

In fact, she has just asked me not to mention this until after Christmas.

CASS

(*unable to hold her own line*): So I left a note for Momma and one for Connie . . .

HARRY

But I said no, definitely no.

CASS

They tell me Connie's a big shot in Dublin now—two department stores and married and all and a chauffeur-driven car . . .

HARRY

And I can tell you that Dom is missing none of your antics, and at his impressionable age, too.

CASS

So I left a note for him, see; one for him and one for Momma; but he must never have gotten his.

HARRY

But that's all finished, all finished. And to get back to my decision—

CASS *cannot fight the memory any longer. She suddenly wheels wildly around to him. She almost screams her lines.*

CASS

Say out what you're trying to say, Harry! Speak up and say it out straight!

HARRY

Cass, I've come to the decision—

CASS

Well?

ALICE *appears at the door left,* DOM *and* MOTHER *at the door right.* CASS's *volume drops rapidly.*

HARRY

I've arranged for you to go into Eden House next Monday.

CASS

Where?

HARRY

It's a rest home for elderly people, at the end of the town, near the black church.

ALICE

Harry, I asked you to wait until—

CASS

That the workhouse?

HARRY

It's where the workhouse used to be.

ALICE

There's no urgency, Cass. You can stay with us—over Christmas.

CASS

(*incredulous*): Jeez, the work—

HARRY

It's not the workhouse. It's a rest home.

CASS

(*totally broken*):   I'm not going.

HARRY

Every week the bank will pay your board and send you an allowance.

CASS

I'm not going.

ALICE

They're very particular about who they take in there, Cass.

HARRY

And you're under no obligation whatever to me. You're entirely independent.

CASS

I haven't a dime.

HARRY

Your own money will support you adequately.

CASS

I haven't a dime.

HARRY

It's all intact.

CASS

I'm not going.

ALICE

Any time you feel like coming out to visit us . . .

CASS

(*in desperation*): Momma . . . ?

MOTHER

You'll remember this day.

CASS

Dommie boy . . . ?

DOM

I'll call on my way from school every—

HARRY

Dom! You're too sensible to make a scene, Cass.

She surveys them slowly. Pause.

CASS

Next Monday?

ALICE

I think we should wait until after—

HARRY

Next Monday. It's all settled.

CASS *turns her back on them and talks to the audience. She is very still, very subdued. The brashness has vanished.*

CASS

(*searching for any words*): Monday for wealth, Tuesday for health, Wednesday the best day of all; Thursday for crosses, Friday for losses. (*Driving herself into a sort of gaiety*) I wear sneakers, you know, with the toes cut out cos my feet, boy, they sure give me hell standing behind that counter. Fine on a Monday morning, and not too bad on Tuesday, but by Wednesday—Jeez—way up like this; and for the rest of the week they're throbbing like they had the neuralgia. (*The others drift out quietly*) And this doc I go to, boy, is he a comedian, he sez: You gotta spend the mosta the day in a recumbent posture. No filthy cracks, Mister, I sez; in case you haven't noticed I'm a lady, cos I thought he was making his move. But Jeff he told me what the doc meant, and when I knew what it was, I just laughed—you know—serving coffee in a recumbent posture! . . . Hell, this is no fun for you, huh? No way to make friends and influence people. The Loves of Cass McGuire—huh! Where did he get that title from anyways? (*Rising to her feet. As if confused*) Where have all the real people gone?

INGRAM

(*off reading*): At that time young Tristan lived at the court of his uncle, King Mark.

Immediately she hears TRILBE *and* INGRAM *approaching,* CASS *pulls open her bag, takes out a compact, and powders herself rapidly.*

CASS

Abbott and Costello again! Maybe they'll give us a laugh.

They enter. INGRAM *is reading from one of the books he always carries, and* TRILBE *is listening to him attentively.*

TRILBE

We've been round three times. I feel positively intoxicated.

CASS

Boy, you're lucky.

INGRAM

And there he captivated everybody with his good looks and his minstrelsy . . .

CASS

Don't he get tired doing the mobile-library act?

TRILBE

(*confidentially*): His Wagner, m'dear. Won't trust them with anyone.

CASS

Wagner?

INGRAM

You know Wagner?

CASS

Do I know Wagner! Voted for him every election.

INGRAM

Elect—?

CASS

Best mayor New York ever had.

TRILBE

There you are. It's a small world, isn't it? By the way, m'dear, what *is* your Christian name?

CASS

Cass.

TRILBE

Cass? Cass? It's certainly not Cass. (*To* INGRAM) Did you ever hear of anyone being christened Cass?

CASS

I was baptized Catherine.

TRILBE

Agh, Catherine! Now we have it! I'll call you Catherine and I insist you call me Trilbe. (*Softly*) His Christian name is Meurice. He is convinced his father did it to him on purpose.

CASS

Couldn't we call him Buster or something?

TRILBE

(*seriously assessing the name*): Buster . . .

CASS

Or what about . . . yeah, Pop! Huh?

TRILBE

I don't think he'd like that, m'dear. He has been Mr. Ingram for so long now. (*Aloud*) Continue reading, Mr. Ingram. (*Softly*) His explosives are very vital.

CASS

Gee . . .

TRILBE

—but his vowels are inclined to be flabby.

CASS

Oh, I'm sorry to hear—

INGRAM

(*irritably*): If you would only keep quiet.

TRILBE

Nobody's saying a word. (*Softly*) I've my adjudication almost ready.

CASS

Yeah?

TRILBE

It should be quite impressive. Shhhhhh.

INGRAM

But in a duel with the warrior Morhol he was seriously wounded and went to Ireland to recuperate.

TRILBE

I can't hear you. Catherine can't hear you. More chest. More lungs.

INGRAM

And there he met Isolde, the daughter of the queen—

TRILBE

Better.

INGRAM

—who ministered to him and tended him and restored him to his former vigor.

CASS

(*to audience*): Jeez, didn't I tell you!

INGRAM

But when his uncle, King Mark, was told of the beauty of Isolde, he dispatched Tristan to fetch Isolde for himself, and Tristan reluctantly set out to do the king's bidding. As he was bringing her back by boat, both he and Isolde drank by mistake the potion which was to make them inseparable lovers.

CASS

(*to audience*): What the hell's keeping Pat Quinn with my potion of hooch!

TRILBE

(*cozily*): It's the part about the exile I like best.

INGRAM

The king married Isolde, and although his spies were constantly on the lookout, she and Tristan met frequently in secret. But finally the king learned of their trysts and exiled Tristan to the coast of Brittany.

TRILBE

Ah!

INGRAM

And there he married another Isolde, but his love was always for the first, the Irish, Isolde. Eventually, having been wounded again—

CASS

(*to audience*): That guy should ov bought hisself accident insurance.

At this, TRILBE *gets to her feet and comes over to* CASS. *She has got to play the following sequence at two levels at once: she is her normal, vital self, inquisitive and anxious to help; and at the same time she must convey the first inklings of an "otherness," of the private world she and* INGRAM *have created and take refuge in occasionally.*

TRILBE

M'dear, who *are* you addressing?

CASS

You just carry on. I'm sorta—you know—having an odd word with the folks out there. (*Indicates audience*)

TRILBE

Who?

CASS

The folks.

TRILBE *shades her eyes against the footlights and searches the*

auditorium. She looks back at CASS *and again at the auditorium.*
She sees no one out there.

TRILBE

Catherine, m'dear, we are your only world now. We have
the truth for you.

CASS

Yeah?

TRILBE

Join with us, Catherine, for we have the truth.

CASS

Sure . . . sure . . .

INGRAM

May I?

TRILBE

We know what is real, Catherine.

INGRAM

Does anybody wish to listen?

TRILBE

Mr. Ingram, I'm going to sit in the winged chair.

INGRAM

It's almost lunchtime and—

TRILBE

I haven't sat in it for three whole weeks, and now I wish to remember.

INGRAM

I really think you ought to wait until—

TRILBE

The past, and all the riches I have, and all that nourishes me.

INGRAM

Very well, Miss Costello.

TRILBE

Mr. Ingram knows my story. And I know his. And we tell our stories to one another occasionally when we're alone . . .

She sits in the winged chair. Very gently bring up Wagner's Venusberg music (omit first two minutes of it). TRILBE *and* IN-GRAM *relax into the mood and respond to one another.*

CASS *is not in their sphere. She watches and listens alertly, cautiously, nervously.*

TRILBE

I was called Trilbe because I was born the year the book was published; and father loved it so much—he was so romantic—and he was so fond of Paris. And it was springtime, and he and I were traveling in Provence—

INGRAM

In the South of France.

TRILBE

—and we were spending a few days in Arles when I met him, Gordon—

INGRAM

Gordon McClelland.

TRILBE

—from Edinburgh. And Father was so proper, you know; so proper and so stern, poor Father.

INGRAM

And what is your profession, young man?

TRILBE

I love your daughter, sir; I love your daughter Trilbe.

INGRAM

I see. I see.

TRILBE

Father always said that when he was puzzled. And in the afternoons, when he would go to his room to rest, Gordon and I would walk hand in hand along the country roads—

INGRAM

Between the poplars.

TRILBE

—in the shafts of golden sun; and every so often we would stop, and he would touch my face with his fingertips and whisper to me—

INGRAM

My little golden Trilbe.

TRILBE

And I would tremble with delight at his gentleness and his beauty and his love for me. And when we married we bought a château—

INGRAM

On the banks of the Loire.

TRILBE

—and had servants and music and wine and still days of sun and children with golden hair, named after princes and princesses; and we traveled and traveled and traveled —Russia, India, Persia, Palestine—never stopping, always moving . . .

INGRAM

My little golden Trilbe.

TRILBE

—sleeping in strange beds, eating strange food—

INGRAM

Goodbye . . . goodbye . . .

TRILBE

Traveling, moving, visiting strange places, meeting new people, with Gordon beside me.

INGRAM

My little golden Trilbe.

TRILBE

And the servants and the music and the wine and the travel and the poetry and his love for me and my love for him . . . all so real. My Gordon from Arles on the Loire, my prince from Edinburgh in Provence . . . my father resting in the afternoon, my journeys to the Nile and the Volga, the road to Samarkand, the road, the traveler's road . . .

INGRAM

Trilbe.

TRILBE

Gordon McClelland.

INGRAM

Golden Trilbe.

TRILBE

My highland prince.

INGRAM

My little golden Trilbe.

TRILBE

Say it slowly after me: *But I being poor have only my dreams . . .*

INGRAM

Our truth.

TRILBE

. . I have spread my dreams under your feet.
Tread softly because you tread on my dreams.

INGRAM

Our truth.

TRILBE

Love was his profession. And Father was such a sensible man. (*She rises slowly to her feet and offers her arm to* INGRAM) You may lead me to the dining room, Mr. Ingram.

INGRAM

My pleasure.

*He takes her arm and they exit like a king and his queen. The
music fades with them.*

CASS *stares in naked astonishment after them. She is still gaping
at the exit left when* DOM *appears in the shadows right. She does
not turn to face him but answers him automatically: she is still
thinking of what has happened.*

DOM

Psst! Auntie Cass!

CASS

Hi . . .

DOM

Did you live with Jeff Olsen, the man that owned the
place you worked in, Auntie Cass?

CASS

(*nodding yes*): Poor good Jeff . . . lost a leg in the
Great War . . .

DOM

Were you ever married to him?

CASS

Had a wife somewhere on the West Coast . . .

DOM

Did you sleep with him?

CASS

And when the pain in the missing leg got real bad, I stroked his forehead . . . (*At this,* DOM *laughs coarsely and darts into the wings.* CASS *turns around front. Calling softly, vaguely*) Jeff? . . . Jeff? . . . Connie?

Enter PAT *left.*

PAT

I could smell the bacon out on the street. Boys but I could eat a horse.

CASS

Hi, Pat . . .

PAT

Are you all right? There's nothing wrong with you, is there?

CASS

Pat, tell me, Pat, what did her father do?

PAT

Whose father?

CASS

Trilbe Costello's.

PAT

He was a French polisher by trade, but he couldn't hold

a job. Never sober. Ended up as a sort of a caretaker out at the greyhound track. Always wore Wellingtons and a greasy bowler hat. Your mother could tell you all about—

CASS

Did she travel?

PAT

Didn't I tell you! Never lit—running from one school to the next, and hoping for a square meal.

CASS

Or married—was she ever married to a guy from Scotland?

PAT

For God's sake, woman, she wouldn't know the difference between a bull and a clucking hen! What the hell's come over you?

CASS

I dunno, Pat. Jeez, I dunno.

PAT

You're foundered with the cold. Here's the stuff'll put some life into you. (*Produces bottle*)

CASS

Yeah . . . yeah . . . phew!

PAT

Have you a glass in your bag?

CASS

I don't need a glass. Boy, is this a gook joint! Jeez, a girl would want to have her wits about her here! (*To audience*) Gordon! What d'you know! Almost had me fooled, too. (*To* PAT) But I can handle gooks—spent a lifetime handling gooks. Skid Row, I'll tell you, it was full of them, full of them . . . (*She drinks from the bottle*) And I'll handle this, too, Pat, huh?

PAT *is watching her cautiously. He decides it is best to humor her, just as he did earlier with* TRILBE.

PAT

Here's your change.

CASS

Keep it. You bet, they'll not wear Cass McGuire down, huh?

PAT

You're looking better already.

CASS

No siree. I'll ride this gook joint.

PAT

Now you're talking.

CASS

By Jeez, I'll ride it, Pat, huh?

PAT

That's fighting language!

CASS

And I'll beat it, too, Pat.

PAT

I'm with you there.

CASS

We'll beat it together, Pat!

PAT

Up the Republic!

CASS

Together, Pat, we'll beat it, boy! It'll not get us down. No siree!

QUICK CURTAIN

ACT TWO

When the curtain rises, CASS *is sitting on her bed, making up Christmas parcels. A miniature Christmas tree sits on the pillow. She is smoking and has a bottle at hand. She talks directly to the audience.*

CASS

Hi, I made damn sure to be in possession this time. I'll tell you. And I hope you don't get the flu from me cos nearly everybody in this joint got it—even matron; and, boy, the bug that put her on her back deserves a citation. Buster Ingram, he got it too, and Pat, and most of the folks in the upper wing. Me—I took precautions. (*Drinks*) But the whole house is kinda depressed, you know. That's why I fixed this (*tree*) up for the common room and bought a couple of presents. Not that I ever went in for this Christmas schmaltz. Hell, we open Christmas morning at 5:30, same as usual; probably the busiest morning in the whole year; and the stream of poor bastards coming howling for black coffee—you should ov seen them! Happy Christmas—Jeez! (*Softly*) But one Christmas night, nineteen and forty-two it was, Jeff and me we're sitting listening to the radio or something, and Jeff he jumps up and sez, "Hell, Cass, I almost forgot!" and he hobbles into the kitchen and comes back with this tiny box, and he sez, "Here," like it was burning him; and I opens it, and there's this brooch, made like it was a shamrock, with three leaves and all, and with green and white and orange diamonds plastered all over it—only they were glass, I guess. And, hell, I dunno what happened to me; maybe I was drunk or something; but I began to cry. And poor Jeff he didn't know where to look, and he shouted, "Jeez, Cass, I gave some Irish bum a ham and cheese sandwich for it day before yesterday. You don't think I *bought* it?" And, Gawd, I cried all the more then . . . must ov been real drunk . . . you know, he was so kind to me . . . (*Raucously*) Hell, I hate Sundays!

Enter TESSA *with brush and dustpan.* CASS *hides the bottle.*

TESSA
Look at the mess the floor's in!

CASS
I'll clean it up.

TESSA
Some people were reared in a byre. (*Picks up one of the presents, a spray of artificial flowers*) Aw, isn't that lovely!

CASS

Like it?

TESSA

They're nicer than real.

CASS

Yeah.

TESSA

And I have a pink dress, too.

CASS

Well . . .

TESSA

Would you ever?

CASS

What?

TESSA

Give them to me.

CASS

(*gently*): Sweetie, I wouldn't give you the time of day.

TESSA

You dirty, mean aul' pagan! (*So refined*) Thanks be to God *I* was at Mass this morning.

She swaggers off and CASS *watches her with amusement.*

CASS

There goes a walking saint. It's (*the flowers*) for Trilbe; and these gloves are for Buster Ingram; and I got socks (*holds one up*) for Pat. I thought they went in pairs, these things. (*She finds the other*) They do. Poor guy, always talking about that nephew of his taking him away. Some nephew, I'll tell you. Which reminds me of something he was telling me the other day: Ingram's married! What d'you know about that! (*Looks around before she continues*) He was only a young guy, see, slashing away at the organ in this swank English cathedral, and this day in comes this hoofer from a nearby music hall—you know —a dancer, flinging her legs up and making guys sweat. Anyways, Buster he sees her and falls hard for her and can't let her outa his sight, not even for a second . . . (*Checking mentally: this has not occurred to her before*) But I ask you, what the hell was the hoofer doing in the swank cathedral in the first place? Mebbe her feet were hurting her. Anyways, old hot-rod Ingram he throws up the organ bashing and follows the variety troupe she's in all over England! And his father—he was a judge or something—he goes chasing after Buster; and his momma she goes chasing after his father. Must ov been like the Keystone Cops. But finally in some hick town on the Coast he gets her to marry him. And two days after the wedding, what does she do? Sails off with some German count that

has a yacht there! Never seen her again. How about that!
(*Trailing off vaguely*) I guess it was the title tickled her
. . . and the yacht . . . Count and Countess . . . Countess Connie . . . the bastard! Anyways, she sailed away,
and forgot everything and never came back again, and
maybe that's what I should ov done. But I came back to
Ireland and got such a welcome that, Jeez, I thought for
ten minutes I was Santa Claus!

HARRY *enters. He is wearing slippers and is dressed in a cardigan.
He has just had his evening meal and is relaxed. He sits beside
the fire.* CASS *continues to address the audience.*

HARRY
Lord, it really is wonderful, Cass, to have you back. I—I
just can't believe it!

CASS
She was a hoofer, but what the hell was her name . . . ?

HARRY
The trouble is, I've so much to tell you and so much to
ask you that I don't know where to begin.

CASS
Anyways, she sailed away forever . . .

HARRY
Fifty-one years—my God, it's a lifetime.

CASS

Fifty-two.

HARRY

And yet I distinctly remember the morning you went away. I ran up to the back attic—remember the back attic with the window you pushed open with the iron bar?

CASS

Six slots in it . . .

HARRY

And I threw myself across your bed and cried my heart out.

CASS

Harry . . . I don't want to remember.

HARRY

D'you know, I was convinced my heart was literally crushed!

CASS

Please . . . please, Harry, let me forget.

HARRY

We were always so close to one another, Cass. Always. I thought the sun rose and set on you. Welcome home a thousand times.

Now, for the first time, CASS *wheels around and almost runs into the common room. She is ecstatic with joy. She wanders about the common room, looking at it, looking at* HARRY, *laughing foolishly.*

CASS

Home! I can't even begin to tell you what this means to me, Harry. This is what it was all for—to come home again. You and Alice and the kids . . . Jeez, Harry, I hope it's not too much for me—you know—like a highball on an empty stomach.

HARRY

We'll make up for all the lost years, Cass.

CASS

And what a home. I'm so glad for you, Harry, I can't tell you.

Enter ALICE *with a tray of drinks.*

CASS

(continued): And Alice! You know you're just like you are in all those pictures. Hell, you were only—what?—a polliwog in a cot when I left, but I knew your father okay.

ALICE

Everybody knew Father.

CASS

Joe Connor? For Gawd's sakes every evening when we'd

be coming home from school we'd meet him at the court-house steps and he'd call one of us over and . . . (*suddenly realizing*) and . . . and he'd say, "How are youse, girls?" . . . Oh, a real gentleman, Mr. Connor, with his gold chain across here and his butterfly collar—

ALICE

You must be exhausted after the flight. Would you try a little sherry?

CASS

I'll try anything—whisky for preference. Tell me, how's the kids?

ALICE

Great.

CASS

When am I going to see them?

ALICE

We don't see a lot of them ourselves, but they'll all come flocking now.

CASS

Father Tom still teaching away at the high school?

ALICE

Didn't you know? He's left the seculars. In the Jays now.

CASS

Yeah?

ALICE

For the past three and a half years.

CASS

Gawd! Can't the docs do nothing for him?

HARRY

The Jays—the Jesuits, Cass.

CASS

Jeez, I thought she said the jakes!

HARRY

I'm going to propose a toast.

CASS

Lovely!

HARRY

To Cass and to the future.

CASS

I'll drink to that.

HARRY

And I want to say this, too: this is your home now, Cass; look on yourself as one of the family.

ALICE

Come and go as you wish.

CASS

And I want to propose a toast. (*Recalling*) Hold on now
—Shocht sleacht an shliocht do shleachta.

ALICE

German?

CASS

Hell, it's supposed to be gawddam Gaelic, and it means—
I forget—May your offspring have offspring—or something.

HARRY

Why did you never marry out there?

CASS

Me?

ALICE

We often thought you might have married the proprietor
of the restaurant you were manageress in.

CASS

The rest—? Oh, Jeff Olsen! Hell, Jeff and me were too
pally to get married, you know. A sweet guy, but as I used
to say to him: "Jeff, boy, I want a man with his two feet
on the ground."

HARRY

He was a successful businessman, wasn't he?

CASS

Sure. But he had only one leg. Who's for more swill? (*She pours herself another drink*)

ALICE

Did you mention the party to her?

HARRY

I didn't have a chance yet.

CASS

What's that?

HARRY

We were talking of having a welcome-home party for you.

CASS

Wonderful! I can still dance . . . (*She lifts her skirt and does a few steps of an old-time waltz as she hums her own accompaniment*) And I'll sing, by Gawd, if the neighbors don't object! (*Sings*)

"Oft in the stilly night ere slumber's chains have bound me Sad memory brings the light . . ."

Aw, hell, I haven't sang since the night James Michael Curley was buried!

ALICE

You're a caution, Cass.

CASS

This party—who's coming?

HARRY

We'll have the Traynors and the Kirks and the Grahams
and Tom and Mary—

CASS

Do I know any of these folk?

HARRY

Course you do. Remember old Jack Kirk out at the end of
the town?

CASS

Yeah, sure.

HARRY

Well, this is his son and his wife. And d'you remember
Goldpark Lodge?

CASS

Colonel Johnson's place? He's not alive, is—?

HARRY

No, no; the Grahams bought it.

CASS

The whole estate? Boy, they must be swank, huh?

ALICE

They own a dance hall here. (*To* HARRY) Is that swank?

HARRY

And the Dohertys and the Tobins and the Wallaces—

CASS

(*too casually*): I don't know none of them. But I'll pitch in. Any of the Crowleys knocking about still?

ALICE

I don't think so.

HARRY

Crowleys? No, moved to Dublin—oh, years ago. Con married a girl from there. Did very well for himself, too. And we'll have the Doyles and Bill Morgan and—

CASS *is moving around the room again, staring in admiration.*

CASS

Boy, Harry, you made out good, huh?

HARRY

Not bad, Cass.

CASS

And you tell me you don't work at the accountancy no more?

HARRY

Not for fifteen, twenty years. I didn't have the time.

CASS

Gee, I'm so glad for you. I was always worried in case— you know—with Momma living with you and all and the kids getting education—like I thought you mebbe didn't have much to fling around. But this! Boy!

ALICE *whispers to* HARRY.

HARRY

I wasn't much of a letter writer, Cass.

CASS

You were just great, Harry. (*To* ALICE) You know he actually wrote me when Father died. Wasn't that something?

HARRY

I know, I know, I know, and I apologize.

CASS

If it hadn't ov been for you (ALICE), the whole family might ov been—in the Jays.

HARRY

And I should have written to thank you for all the money you sent; every month without fail.

CASS

Forget it.

HARRY

No, I won't forget it. And I want to talk to you about it now.

ALICE

We never really thanked you properly.

CASS

I had no use for it.

HARRY

Only this morning I was checking up: ten dollars every month for fifty-two years—

ALICE

Not to talk of the children's birthdays and Christmas presents and—

CASS

I couldn't help making it. Honest. It just kept dropping into my lap.

HARRY

There would have been no point in telling you we really didn't need it; you would have sent it all the same.

CASS

Not now, Harry. (*Looking around again*) It's—it's elegant—that's what it is.

HARRY

Thank God we were never in want. In the beginning Mother's salary was adequate, and then I qualified and went into practice, and I had a few lucky ventures.

CASS

I would only have scattered it anyways.

HARRY

What troubles me now, though, is that perhaps you were the one who needed it, and not us.

CASS

It got candy for the kids, didn't it?

ALICE

Don't keep her in suspense. Tell her what you did.

CASS

I sent a few bucks cos I wanted to. So forget it. Okay?

HARRY

I checked this morning. And over the years—including birthdays, anniversaries, Christmas, and all—you sent 7,419 dollars—something over two and a half thousand pounds. And that's not counting interest.

Enter DOM *and* MOTHER. *They stay upstage.*

CASS

Boy, that would ov bought me one hellova head! Momma, how are you, Momma? Kid.

HARRY

Don't think we don't appreciate the sacrifices you made. We do, all of us—

CASS

(*to* MOTHER): Tell him to shut up, will you? He's boring the hell outa me.

HARRY

No, this must be said. When you went out there first, ten dollars must have been a lot of money.

CASS

(*getting really tired*): Harry—

HARRY

However, to get back to what I was saying: we saved it for you, Cass.

CASS

?

HARRY

It was all banked, every penny of it from the very beginning. As I said, we never really needed it. And now it's
all intact, for you to use as you wish.

ALICE

It's a nice little nest egg.

HARRY

And it makes you independent of everyone.

ALICE

We've been planning this as a surprise.

HARRY

How you're fixed financially is your own affair, but this
will provide a nice supplement to whatever you have. I'll
give you the passbook tomorrow morning.

ALICE

And I'm warning you to keep an eye on this scrounger
(DOM). Don't let him wheedle a halfpenny from you!

CASS

(*almost whispering*):   None of it . . . never bought nothing?

HARRY

If we had needed it. But, thank God, we never did. The important thing is not the money itself, Cass—it's not all that much—but the knowledge that you are not dependent on anyone. That's what it gives you.

CASS

Dependent?

HARRY

You can crack your fingers at all of us!

CASS

The kids' birthdays . . . and the doc's bills . . . and Father Tom's education . . . ?

HARRY

I assure you, Cass, we never wanted for anything. And we're as grateful as if we had used it.

CASS *walks away from them. She is slowly trying to take in what she has been told. Pause.*

ALICE

Cass . . . ?

CASS

I could ov bought myself a mink coat! So! I could ov put

a fan in the bedroom in the summer! Yeah! Another thing
—I could ov eaten prime beef every Sunday!

ALICE

We thought you'd be delighted.

CASS *wheels around on them, madly, desperately elated. She speaks
almost at full voice.*

CASS

There was only one story would make Jeff laugh—you
know? Brave as a lion, but, Jeez, that leg of his gave him
hell at times; and when he would get away down there he
would say to me, "Tell me the story about the Irish mick,
Cass." And I would stroke his forehead and tell him, see,
and he would laugh and laugh even though he heard that
story hundreds—millions of times—

MOTHER

This is indeed a festive occasion.

CASS

Boy, is she psychic! You know the story, Alice? About
this Irish kid comes over to the States, see, and after three
months he writes back to the folks: "I've been made floor
manager of this store. This is a feather in my cap." And
the folks back home they're thrilled, see, even though
there's no dough in the envelope. And three months later

he writes again: "I've been made manager of the whole plant. This is a feather in my cap." Again no dough, but the folks is pleased for him, see. And three months later another letter: "I've been made president of the company. This is a feather in my cap."

HARRY *laughs—an attempt at normality.* CASS *almost spits her anger at him.*

CASS

You haven't heard the punch line yet! What the hell are you laughing at?

HARRY

I just thought—president after nine months—

CASS

And then they don't hear from the kid for months and months, see, not a line; until finally they get this air letter, very urgent, and written inside is: "I'm broke. Please send fare home." And the kid's pop he gets pen and paper, and he clears the kitchen table, and he writes back: "Stick the three feathers up your ass and fly home!"

Only DOM *laughs.* ALICE *turns to him rapidly.*

ALICE

Take Mother to her room at once!

Exit DOM *and* MOTHER.

HARRY

Cass, this sort of—

CASS

When you planning to have this party? I'll supply the champagne—I got money, haven't I? And I'll sing and dance and I'll tell stories and I'll have all the Kirks and Colonel Johnson and all the Crowleys and all of them rolling in the aisles. (*To* ALICE, *who is about to leave with the tray of drinks*) Come back with that hooch, honey! I'm only warming up!

ALICE *leaves*.

HARRY

Cass—

CASS

I got more stories than Bennett Cerf ever heard of—about cannibals and girls with Chinese tattooes on their bellies and about elephants and marooned sailors—hell, that's all Slinger ever done was tell me stories. He was a bum, okay, but he had lovely teeth. Like the one about this guy that comes home drunk every night and his wife she's about sick of him. You know that one, Harry?

HARRY

Cass, this sort of talk—

CASS

So sick she can't stick it no more. Anyways, this night the guy comes home plastered again and falls across the bed and starts snoring. And the wife she has this empty candy box with a great big blue satin rosette on the lid, and she takes the rosette off the box and goes over to the bed and takes the guy's trousers off and ties the bow to his rice crispies. And the next morning when he wakes up first thing he sees is this big blue rosette. And the wife she says to him, "Where were you last night?" And the guy he scratches his head and he says, "Jeez, honey, I don't know. But wherever I was I got first prize."

HARRY

I'll speak to you later, Cass.

He marches off. CASS, *left alone, suddenly slumps into a chair. The false elation is all gone, the anger all dead. She is on the verge of tears.*

CASS

I never wanted no gawddam mink coat! And I hate prime beef! And fans they give me the sinus! As for air conditioning—Gawd—you can keep it, keep it . . . I don't want it . . . not a cent of it! . . . (*Fumbles for cigarettes, her hands shaking*) Some guy, Slinger, I'll tell you, some helluva guy . . . (*Lights cigarette. Shades her eyes against the lights and searches the auditorium*) You still out there? Stick around and we'll have fun together. You'll see, lots of fun . . . (*Looking around set*) Where the hell *is* everybody? (*To audience*) You wanta know why I never got married? Cos I hadn't time—that's the why—working—and then I sorta fell in with Jeff, and we had our own arrangement. He was no sweet guy but he liked me—I know he did—he never said it but I know he did. And when he died, well what d'you do but come home . . . That's what it's all about, isn't it—coming home? Why the hell does he call it "The Loves of Cass McGuire"? A gook title, I'll tell you!

She hears TRILBE *approach and takes out her compact and makes up. While she does this, she keeps her back to* TRILBE.

CASS

Hi.

TRILBE

Catherine, m'dear, what are you doing?

CASS

(*brisk, busy*): Getting ready for the ball.

TRILBE

Are we having a ball?

CASS

Why not. Where's Fred Astaire?

TRILBE

I beg your pardon?

CASS

Mr. Ingram—he not about?

TRILBE

He's in the chapel.

CASS

Got religion all of a sudden?

TRILBE

Catherine, I think you should know: today is the anniversary of his wife's death.

This shocks CASS *into normality. Pause.*

CASS

Gee, I didn't know she was *dead*.

TRILBE

Very tragic. Very, very tragic.

CASS

When did it happen to her?

Enter INGRAM, CASS *stares at him.*

TRILBE

Some other time . . . (*Briskly*) Tell us about the catering business in America, Catherine.

CASS

(*watching* INGRAM): Sure, sure, it was something . . . you bet . . . I worked in this . . . this downtown restaurant . . . you know, all big shots; and I was . . . sort of like a headwaiter, only I was a woman, you know . . . Hi, Mr. Ingram.

TRILBE

That must have been fascinating employment.

CASS

You bet . . . yeah . . . Mr. Ingram . . .

INGRAM

Good afternoon.

CASS

Mr. Ingram, it has just come to my knowledge that you are bereaved of your spouse . . .

INGRAM

Yes. Yes.

CASS

And I would like you to understand that I am deeply grieved on your behalf.

INGRAM

It was a long time ago.

CASS

Was it the TB or the cancer, Mr. Ingram? Jeez, the number of women I know that went down with the cancer—boy, you could ov packed Radio City with them.

TRILBE

I think it is milder today, don't you?

INGRAM

Stella was drowned, Miss McGuire.

CASS

Gawd.

INGRAM

Forty-six years ago. I will tell you about it.

He moves towards the winged chair and sits.

TRILBE

Mr. Ingram—

INGRAM

On our honeymoon.

TRILBE

Mr. Ingram, dear, should you . . . today . . . ?

INGRAM

I will tell you about it.

TRILBE

Very well then.

Gently fade in Wagner's "Magic Fire" music. Then, after a few seconds, INGRAM *continues.*

INGRAM

I was twenty, and she was eighteen, with hair golden as ripe wheat—

TRILBE

A ballet dancer.

INGRAM

And after the wedding we went to Salcombe—

TRILBE

In Devon, in the South of England.

INGRAM

And every night in the hotel I played the piano and she danced and danced and danced—

TRILBE

Her hair swinging behind her.

INGRAM

And I played and played, faster and faster—

TRILBE

For her dancing, dancing.

INGRAM

Until her eyes shone with happiness and the room swam with delight and my heart sang with joy—

TRILBE

Oh, the dancing, dancing.

INGRAM

And during the day we walked across the moors—

TRILBE

Hand in hand.

INGRAM

—and kissed and loved and ran and danced—

TRILBE

Across the windy moors.

INGRAM

—because my prize was a young prize, with hair golden as ripe wheat; and there was music in my ears, throbbing, heady, godly music . . .

TRILBE

Away, away to the end of the promontory.

INGRAM

Where we kissed and danced and loved . . .

TRILBE

Poised above the waves.

INGRAM

And then—

TRILBE

And then—

INGRAM

And then, one day, running before me, calling to me, she slipped . . .

TRILBE

His Stella—

INGRAM

And there was no sound.

TRILBE

His star.

INGRAM

No sound but the sound of the sea. And for nine days they searched—

TRILBE

Probing with long poles.

INGRAM

—from a German yacht that was fishing there; he was a prince.

TRILBE

His dancing Stella.

INGRAM

Swirling in the water, loose, being nosed by fish, her hair loose, her limbs loose . . .

TRILBE

His dancing star.

INGRAM

But they never found her. And the German yacht sailed away—

TRILBE

On a spring morning.

INGRAM

—away to the Mediterranean, to the sun . . . with hair golden as ripe wheat.

TRILBE

Leaving them together, in Salcombe, in the South of England.

INGRAM

My prize, my bride . . .

TRILBE

His dancing bride.

INGRAM

My dancing, swirling bride.

TRILBE

Our truth.

INGRAM

But I being poor have only my dreams—

TRILBE

I have spread my dreams under your feet—

INGRAM

Tread softly because you tread on my dreams.

TRILBE

Our truth.

They hold their positions for a few seconds; then INGRAM *rises.*

INGRAM

It is such a mild afternoon . . . I . . . I think we'll walk past the refectory and along . . . it's a very pleasant little . . .

He goes towards the door.

TRILBE

A splendid idea. Wait for me, Mr. Ingram. (*She goes with him, but hesitates before she exits, and turns to* CASS) Join with us, Catherine. Join with *us.*

They go off. Fade out music. CASS *stares after them. Her reaction this time is not too violent. She is more perplexed, more puzzled. She talks to herself.*

CASS

Jee-sus! What d'you know about that! (*Fumbling for a cigarette*) As if those Germans couldn't find a needle in a haystack, for Gawd's sake! (*To audience: far from confident*) Hi! . . . Stick . . . stick around . . . This'll be okay, you'll see; this'll all sort itself out . . . I dunno . . . this gawddam going back into the past! Who the hell knows what happened in the past! Joe Bolowski, he

thought he was a gawddam pianist! . . . Jeez, how do
I know . . . maybe he was . . .

ALICE *appears in the shadows upstage.* CASS *does not look at her,
and her answers are automatic.*

ALICE

My father was always a gentleman, Cass, wasn't he?

CASS

Sure . . . sure . . .

ALICE

There were rumors, malicious rumors, about him; but they
weren't true, Cass, were they?

CASS

A gentleman, honey. That was Joe Connor.

ALICE

But there were whispers, and they were carried to me
after his death.

CASS

One of the most respected men in town.

ALICE

He was, wasn't he?

CASS

Sure.

ALICE

And dignified, and scholarly, and courteous?

CASS

You can say that again.

ALICE

(*grandly*): Yes, of course he was. One of the old families.

CASS

Old as the Hudson.

ALICE

Yes, the old gentility. They may not have had wealth, but they had background. And background's so important.

She disappears into the wings.

CASS

(*turns, appealing*): Alice, honey . . . Momma? . . . Harry? . . . Father? . . . Connie, Connie? . . .

She is about to wander into her bedroom when PAT QUINN *makes his usual brisk entrance.*

PAT

Wonderful! Wonderful! Wonderful!

CASS

Pat! Gee, am I glad to see you, Pat! Where you been?

PAT

I told you all along but you never believed me!

CASS

We'll have a party, Pat; and I've got presents to hand out; and I'll get Buster Ingram to play the piano and—

PAT

He's coming for me this day week—him and the wife.

CASS

Sure, Pat; you're only temporary—

PAT

You won't believe me. You never did. But he's just after leaving the door. He took my trunk away with him. Look —the receipt from the matron: "Paid with thanks." A split new house with a room and all for me. In a week, on his way home from the monthly meeting.

CASS

(*totally deflated*): On the level?

PAT

I knew you never believed me. You thought I was only blathering like yourself. But there it is in black and white. Ask Tessa. She helped me out with the trunk.

CASS

(*with quiet venom*): You dirty bastard!

PAT

Ha-ha-ha-ha-ha, we see the true colors now! The big swank American lady, Mr. McGuire's sister. Ah but you never fooled me, McGuire. A skivvy—that's what you were— written all over you. And a drunken aul skivvy, living in sin with a dirty aul Yank that kicked you out in the end.

CASS

Shut up!

PAT

But what else would you expect. Didn't your aul fella do the same in Scotland. And we know your stuck-up aul mother that never paid a bill in her life. Oho, I know youse all right—tramps turned respectable! Respectable, how are you!

CASS

Shut up!

PAT

Who'll carry you your drink now? Aul raving Costello? Aul mad Ingram? Cripes, you'll be a prize trio. The people'll be paying to come and look at youse!

CASS

Shut up, you bastard! Shut up!

PAT

Oh, the ladylike Miss McGuire! Oh, the sweet lady! Good luck to you! It won't be long till you start raving, too! Rave away, woman! You'll be in good company!

He skips off. CASS, *angry, sobbing, rushes into her room, takes the bottle from under the mattress and drinks. Throughout all this business she is mumbling incoherently to herself. Then she lights a cigarette and then makes up.*

CASS

Jeez, the fun Jeff and me had that day we went to Coney Island . . . Lincoln's Birthday, nineteen and twenty-seven . . . that's when it was . . . we laughed and laughed and laughed, that day on Coney Island . . . Connie . . . Connie . . .

The room is too lonely. She rushes back to the common room. Through the French windows we can see TRILBE: *She beckons to* CASS. CASS, *too, sees her, and swings around to the audience.*

TRILBE

Catherine!

CASS *shades her eyes and searches the auditorium.*

TRILBE

Catherine!

CASS

(*to* TRILBE): Leave me alone, will you? (*To audience*) They think they're going to run me back into the past but by Gawd they're not . . . I live in the present, Harry boy, right here and now. Where are you? Stick with me.

TRILBE

Catherine!

CASS

Go away! Go away! Gooks . . . real gooks living in the past, but not Cass McGuire. (*To audience*) If things get too rough I can go and hide in the signal box. I've always got places I can go to . . . always . . . you bet . . . a dozen of them . . . out to the crooked bridge . . . at the back of the mill . . . But the signal box . . . it's the safest . . . no one ever looks there . . . Where are you? Jeez, where are you?

TRILBE

Catherine!

She now stands strained between the calling voice and the audience. Her mouth forms words, but no sound comes. We wait for her to break down. Then, in a voice that is firm and clear, she calls:

CASS

One black coffee and one salad sandwich? You bet. Coming right up, sir. Coming right up.

QUICK CURTAIN

ACT THREE

The evening of Christmas Eve. CASS *is lying asleep on her bed. She is partially dressed.* TRILBE *and* INGRAM *are sitting at the table. He is writing a letter and she is reading the paper. Silence.*

TRILBE

You are concentrating too deeply on that letter. You'll end up with a headache.

INGRAM

If I could only have a little quiet . . .

TRILBE

I used to suffer from migraine once. (*She reads*) Imagine that!

INGRAM

Mm?

TRILBE

The temperature in Sydney yesterday was ninety-seven degrees.

INGRAM
Really.

TRILBE
I had a brother in Sydney. Peter.

INGRAM
Yes?

TRILBE
A diver.

INGRAM
What did he dive for?

This has never occurred to TRILBE *before.*

TRILBE
I beg your pardon?

INGRAM
What did he dive for?

TRILBE
How would I know what he dived for, Mr. Ingram. He was a diver—a diver—a diver. And a professional diver—just dives, doesn't he?

INGRAM
I . . . I . . . I suppose so . . .

She goes on reading. He goes on writing. CASS, *without opening her eyes, stretches out a hand, feels under the mattress, finds a bottle, puts it to her mouth. The bottle is empty. The hand throws it away. She drops off again.*

TRILBE

A report of Brother O'Rourke's funeral. Two bishops and three ministers of state.

INGRAM

Who's that?

TRILBE

I told you about him yesterday. Principal of Fairhill Secondary School. A Kerryman. A very . . . athletic principal.

INGRAM

I remember.

TRILBE

"He is survived by three sisters and three broth—" Surely that's a misprint!

INGRAM

Hm?

TRILBE

I presume it should read three sisters and three brothers. He would never have left three brothels, would he?

Enter TESSA *with a notebook and pencil. She is looking very much more alive and quite smart.*

TESSA

Matron says would youse rather a concert or a fillim to-morrow night?

INGRAM

I . . . I really don't . . .

TRILBE

A concert or a film; let us analyze this. Who would be the artists in the concert?

TESSA

How would I know. The fillim is called—

TRILBE

Film, child. One syllable. Film.

TESSA

—General Custer's Last Stand.

TRILBE

That sounds familiar. (*To* INGRAM) Who was General Custer?

INGRAM

Wasn't he one of the leaders of your Easter Rebellion?

TRILBE
I do believe you're right. (*To* TESSA) Yes, I vote for the film.

INGRAM
So do I.

TESSA *holds out her left hand.*

TESSA
And none of youse noticed.

TRILBE
What?

TESSA
Look.

TRILBE
Chilblains, m'dear?

TESSA
I'm engaged. He gave it to me last night.

TRILBE
Well I'm delighted. I wish you every happiness.

INGRAM *rises from the table, goes over to* TESSA, *takes her hand, and kisses her fingers. Throughout this brief ceremony* TESSA *is at first embarrassed, then giggles, and then is oddly moved. As he does this*:

INGRAM

May I? (*Kiss*) A long and contented life to both of you.

TESSA

He's a building contractor by trade.

TRILBE

A very practical profession, too.

TESSA

Well, he's not a real contractor, yet.

TRILBE

But he's a fully fledged tradesman?

TESSA

He will be when he finishes his apprenticeship, and until he sets up on his own he's working as a bricklayer for Harvey and Todd. But he's going to go out on his own in the spring . . . after we're married.

INGRAM

That will be very . . . he'll do well, I'm . . .

TESSA

And the first thing he's going to do is build a bungalow

for us, with bay windows and venetian blinds, and a big garage and a red tiled roof. I think a red roof's nice.

TRILBE

Indeed.

TESSA

We have a site and all in our head but we're not telling anybody where it is in case the price would be stuck up. And as soon as we're settled in comfortable, I want youse two and Miss McGuire to come out and have high afternoon tea with us.

TRILBE

That will be something to look forward to.

TESSA

We're going to do all the entertaining before the babies start coming. I'll put Miss McGuire down for the fillim, too. (*At door*) The aul woman to fill Pat Quinn's place has just arrived. Her name's Lizzie Butcher. She's crying her eyes out. Wouldn't you think at her age she wouldn't mind where she'd be?

She goes swinging off. There is a flatness after her departure, the first of a series that drain the atmosphere of all life and buoyancy. INGRAM *and* TRILBE *return without interest to their tasks.*

TRILBE

Bungalows are all very well if you are positioned on a rise. Otherwise there is no privacy.

INGRAM

They'll have venetian blinds, she said.

TRILBE

You're quite right.

Pause

TRILBE

(*continued*): She must be resting. I haven't seen her all day. Have you?

INGRAM

Have I what?

TRILBE

You can be so stupid at times! Have you seen Catherine?

INGRAM

No . . . no . . . I haven't.

TRILBE

(*hesitantly*): Did you get the impression last night, Mr. Ingram, did it occur to you that Catherine was slashed?

INGRAM

Good heavens! Slashed?

TRILBE

Inebriated. Did that occur to you?

INGRAM

Miss McGuire? Certainly not. I would be very shocked.
(*Pause*) What made you think so?

TRILBE

Nothing. Nothing at all. Probably I imagined it.

INGRAM

I'm certain you did.

TRILBE

Very well. I did. Let's not discuss it any further.

They continue reading and writing. Then suddenly TRILBE *has a
revelation.*

TRILBE

Pearls!

INGRAM

?

TRILBE

That's what people dive for! That's what Peter dived for!

Peter dived for pearls. Round the rugged rocks the ragged rascals ran. My brother Peter dived for precious pearls. Little Tessa should practice on that type of exercise.

HARRY, ALICE, *and* DOM *enter, dressed for an outing. They carry presents.*

HARRY

We're looking for Miss McGuire. Matron said she would be here.

TRILBE *and* INGRAM *pay no attention.*

HARRY

(*continued*): Excuse me . . .

TRILBE

Good evening. Very cold, isn't it?

ALICE

Where could we find Miss McGuire?

TRILBE

We haven't seen Miss McGuire all day, have we, Mr. Ingram?

INGRAM

That's . . . that's what we were just saying.

HARRY

Would she be in her bedroom? I'm her brother.

INGRAM
> Her bedroom is just down the passage.

HARRY
> (*to Alice*):   I'll see is she awake first.

HARRY *goes down front.* DOM *follows him at a distance.*

ALICE
> We brought a few chocolates for all the inma— for all the residents.

TRILBE
> Do you know Brother O'Rourke, m'dear?

ALICE
> I've heard my sons talk of him.

INGRAM
> Thank you for the—

TRILBE
> Well, he's dead, and we're puzzled by the report of his funeral. He had three sisters; that we know; but what we wish to establish is this: had he any brothers?

ALICE, INGRAM, *and* TRILBE *go into mute conversation.* HARRY *stands beside* CASS's *bed. He speaks to her in a quiet, tender voice.* DOM *stands at a distance, tense, alert.*

HARRY

Cass. Cass. It's me, Cass. Harry.

CASS *stirs slowly, then sits up. Automatically gropes for cigarettes, lights one with shaking hands. She looks and feels a wreck. Stares vaguely at her immediate surroundings on stage. Talks listlessly to herself.*

CASS

Where the hell is everyone?

HARRY

Cass . . .

CASS

Gone . . . gone . . .

HARRY

It's Harry, Cass. Alice is outside. We brought a few things for you. Slippers. Fruit.

CASS

Boy, what a dream. Like it kinda went on and on every time I closed my eyes . . .

HARRY

You're very comfortable here. And it's so cold outside. Snow's forecast.

CASS

We're on this big ship, sailing home to Ireland, see . . .
all laughing and singing and dancing and drinking . . .
all the gang of us that used to get up the concerts for the
White Cross and the boys on the run and the church building and the prisoners' fund back home . . . and we're
having that much fun, all sailing for home . . .

HARRY

Cass . . .

CASS

And they're all milling about; and there in the middle of
them—Jeez and was I glad to see them!—there's Joe
Bolowski and Slinger having a ball to theirselves; and
Joe he sees me standing up there in this big long white
wedding dress, and he shouts up to me, "Cass," he shouts,
"I'd pull no chain on that." And everyone laughs and
laughs and laughs, even Father O'Neill. Boy, he should
ov been in the Marines.

HARRY

We're going to have a quiet Christmas after all, Cass. The
children, it seems . . . it seems they can't come. Betty sent
a telegram and Tom phoned this morning. Naturally
they're very disappointed. So I suggested to Alice—

CASS

Gawd, am I hung over!

HARRY

—I was wondering would you like to come out to us for tomorrow . . . and Boxing Day . . . and perhaps for a day or two more . . .

CASS

Jeff he never has a head cos he drinks four pints of iced water before he goes to bed. Sez it makes the alcohol float to the top. Hell, I dunno; but a head's better than running to the ur-eye-nal all night.

HARRY

I'd give you everything I have, Cass, anything, just to be able to put a coat around you and drive you home with me. But when a man gets married . . . and we've had Mother for so long . . . although Alice couldn't have been kinder to her . . .

CASS *swings her feet out of the bed. The effort sets her head throbbing.*

CASS

Oooooh . . . oh-oh-oh . . . Gawd . . . !

HARRY

I don't suppose you know about them, Cass, but she has her worries . . . we both have . . . we haven't heard from Aiden for seven years, not since he went to Switzerland;

she worries a lot about that. And then Betty's marriage isn't just as happy as . . . as . . . Even Tom at times . . . the seculars didn't suit him and we gather that he's restless again even though . . . You really are better off here, Cass.

CASS

During Prohibition there was this hooch called Tiger's Piss. One swig of that stuff and you thought you were Anna May Wong. Oooooooooooh . . . !

HARRY

I'll call again tomorrow. And every week. I promise.

He takes a half bottle of whisky from his pocket and leaves it on the foot of the bed.

CASS

I dunno what I drunk last night. But I guess that tiger's still operating.

HARRY

Goodbye, Cass. A happy Christmas.

He goes reluctantly back to the common room. After he has gone, CASS *finds the bottle he left.*

CASS

Well, I didn't know he had that much foresight.

As she is drinking, DOM darts forward and sticks his face up to CASS's right ear. His eyes are burning with disgust.

DOM

You're nothing but a dirty, rotten, aul— aul— aul—!

He cannot finish. He runs into the common room and then off.

HARRY

Dom? (*Sternly*) Dom!

ALICE

What happened to him?

HARRY

He's probably— Where are you going?

ALICE

I'll only be a minute.

HARRY

There's no point in disturbing her.

ALICE

I'll meet you at the car.

HARRY

For heaven's sake, Alice, she's not—

ALICE

I said I'll only be a minute. See where Dom has gone to.

HARRY *does not want a scene before* TRILBE *and* INGRAM. *He smiles blankly at them, apologetically, and mumbles.*

HARRY

The compliments of the season to you. I'll be in again tomorrow or the next . . .

TRILBE

And a very merry Christmas to you, sir.

HARRY *looks uneasily after* ALICE *and then goes off to find* DOM. ALICE *has moved into* CASS's *bedroom and stands beside her.* CASS *is totally unaware that she is there.*

ALICE

(*warmly, leaning over*): It's me, Cass . . . I know Harry has told you: none of the children . . . (*She checks herself in time, straightens up, continues with a control that is touching in its rigidity. She is on the point of tears*) The children are all coming—all of them—Betty and Tom and Aiden—arriving tonight—late—a real family gathering. You'll like Aiden; he's—you know—unorthodox—his artistic temperament—always moving from job to job— always getting into little scrapes. Oh, you'll love him. And Tom. People say he's like my father; remember? But then Father was a more sort of scholarly man, wasn't he? He'll make an excellent bishop; great administrative ability. And Betty and the baby. We haven't seen it either, you know; our only grandchild. They turned out well, didn't they, Cass? And Harry worked so hard for them.

CASS *makes a quick movement and her head explodes.*

CASS
Jeezus!

ALICE
They're a consolation to us, Cass, aren't they?

CASS
"Oft in the stilly night ere slumber's chains have bound me,
Fond memory brings the light of other days around me."

ALICE *makes a tentative gesture towards* CASS *again.*

ALICE
Cass . . .

CASS
Best mayor New York ever had.

ALICE *withdraws. She dabs at her nose, straightens herself, and dashes out of the bedroom and through the common room.*

TRILBE
And a very happy Christmas to you, too.

ALICE

(*vaguely*): Oh, yes . . . yes . . .

She goes off.

TRILBE

That was Catherine's brother and his wife and their youngest child. They also have a son an architect in U.N.O. and a daughter a doctor, married to a London specialist, and a son a Jesuit.

INGRAM

I'm not deaf, you know.

TRILBE

A very satisfactory family. (*She opens the paper again, then stops*) It's coming back to me now: he led a flying column in Tipperary!

INGRAM

The Jesuit?

TRILBE

General Custer.

CASS *puts on her shoes. She takes a drink and feels better. Completes her dressing. She gets to her feet and is about to go into the common room when she hesitates, takes a few steps towards the footlights, shades her eyes, searches the auditorium. She sees nobody.*

CASS

And I could ov swore there were folks out there. (*Shrugs*)
What the hell.

She shuffles into the common room. TRILBE's *vigor makes her feel
even more sour.*

TRILBE

Ah! There you are!

CASS

Hi.

TRILBE

We've missed you all day. (*Quietly*) He's very upset with
the income-tax people. They have confused him with some
other Meurice Ingram, a professional wrestler.

INGRAM

Good evening.

CASS *waves casually to him.*

TRILBE

And now, Catherine, I want your advice. Where would
be the best place to display my Christmas cards? (*Delving
into bag*) I didn't want to keep them selfishly in my room.
I was thinking of the walls—

CASS

Sure.

TRILBE

—or the mantelpiece. Or what about stringing them across the window? I've got some green tape here, too.

CASS

Yeah, that's fine, fine.

TRILBE

You Americans have such novel ideas about decoration. Here we are! Some of them are so pretty this year.

CASS *takes them listlessly.*

CASS

Five?

TRILBE

There are certainly more than that. (*Searches bag again*) Two more. And I'll get another from Mother Benignus of Loreto. She never has time to do hers until after the Christmas rush. What do you think?

CASS

Well, as the broad said to the senator, you can't— (*Recovering quickly*) —I think mebbe we'll just be old-fashioned and set them up along here (*the mantelpiece*). Okay?

TRILBE

Yes. Yes, perhaps you're right.

CASS *goes downstage and searches for the audience again. Finds no one.*

CASS

No one. Must have been dreaming.

TRILBE

What's that, m'dear?

CASS

The folks—I guess you were right.

TRILBE

Never mind, Catherine, you have us. Our world is real, too.

INGRAM

Our world is just as real.

PAT *comes on singing. He is carrying two cases. He is at the top of his form.*

PAT

Adieu, adieu, kind friends, adieu, adieu, adieu,
I can no longer stay with you, stay with you . . .

The other three go absolutely flat. They watch his antics with dead eyes, almost as if he weren't there.

PAT

(*rapidly*): It has been a pleasure knowing you all. And only that the nephew can't manage without me—he's outside in the car there with the missus, waiting for me— you'd never drag Pat Quinn away from Eden House and the good company and the grand food. Miss Costello, a very happy Christmas to you and the very best of good luck. Mister Ingram, sir, it has been an honor knowing you and being educated by your fine talk. Good luck to you. Miss Mac, we had our differences, Miss Mac, but that's all over and done with. (*Softer*) And if you want me to make an arrangement with Sweeny—you know where— I'm your man, d'you understand?

TESSA

(*at door*): He says if you want to stay that suits him.

PAT

Coming, darling, coming. The season of good will and forgiveness and all; and if ever you want anything done for you outside in the great big world just drop a note to Mister Patrick Joseph Quinn, Esquire, care of Mister John Quinn, Esquire, Cloughmore, and I'll see you right. A happy Christmas, one and all, and a bright and prosperous

New Year, and may all your dreams come true. (*At door*)
By the way, you're getting a slice of ham each for tea.

Exits

The silence now is total, the depression complete. INGRAM *takes
off his glasses and polishes them.* CASS, *her back to the audience,
fingers the cards.* TRILBE *gets a handkerchief and blows her nose
vigorously. Pause. Then high unnatural talk bursts.*

TRILBE

I think perhaps my favorite piece for children is a little
poem I once came across in a magazine during my travels.
It is called "Clickety-clack," and I have recommended it
to dozens of pupils:
*Clickety-clack, clickety-clack, goes the puffing train
on the railway track;
Bearing us off on a mystery tour,
And when we'll arrive we're never quite sure . . .*

INGRAM

When he was a young barrister my father published a
pamphlet attacking capital punishment, and that was . . .
oh, fifty years ago . . . or more . . .

TRILBE

*We puff over meadows and rivers and streams
Till we come, puffing gaily, to the land of our dreams;*

And there we were happy to wander and roam
For we feel so content in this land that is Home . . .

INGRAM

Long, long before the movement ever became popular. He
was a stern man but I think he was a just man . . . in his
own way . . .

TRILBE

We're having ham for tea.

INGRAM

Snow is forecast.

TRILBE

And turkey tomorrow.

INGRAM

I don't suppose it'll lie.

TRILBE

And a film at night.

They cannot sustain talk any longer. Silence flows in and fills
the room. Then, suddenly, CASS *with great effort and courage*
springs into activity.

CASS

Hello! It's Christmas Eve, isn't it? I almost forgot! What

are we all moping for? (*Begins searching in one of her bags*) I got some things in here. Sometimes I think I carry the whole of Macy's around with me! Yeah, yeah, here we are. (*Formally*) Mr. Ingram, a very merry Christmas to you. (*Gives him a parcel*)

INGRAM

Is it—?

CASS

Sure, sure, go ahead. It ain't a Cadillac nor nothing like that. But you might like it.

INGRAM

I haven't had a Christmas present, Miss McGuire, since . . . oh, for . . . for . . .

CASS

Agh, it's nothing; only a pair of— (*She suddenly realizes that she has given him the wrong present. She snatches it back from him again*) Jeez, gimme that back! It's okay, okay, keep calm, keep calm, Father Christmas is still coming; I still got something for you, only I was giving you the wrong thing, see! (*Produces another packet*) And that wouldn't ov been real smart, huh? This is more like it. Yeah, this is it, okay.

INGRAM

I'm deeply moved, Miss McGuire.

CASS

How the hell can you be moved till you see what you got? It ain't no Cadillac neither, I can tell you. Cos they didn't have the color I liked. (*To* TRILBE) I got something for you, too; an accessory for to match along with your pink sweater. Pretty nice.

INGRAM

(*displaying socks*): Thank you very, very much. They're . . . they're . . .

CASS

Yeah, they're a couple of socks. Health to wear. You know like I kinda figured you do a lot of walking past the refectory and along the . . . you know. Only don't bring them back to me to mend. I'm not the sewing type.

The new resident, MRS. BUTCHER, *enters left and walks across stage to the exit right. She is small and old and perky. She is carrying a tiny cardboard case in one hand and a handkerchief in the other. She walks with hesitant courage because she is confused, unsure, timorous, and yet defiant. Because of her uncertainty, her manner appears to be challenging. Immediately at her heels is* TESSA, *carrying her bedclothes.*

TRILBE

Good evening to you.

She looks at TRILBE *and quickly at the others but does not answer and does not slacken her pace. When she goes off,* TESSA *puts her head back again.*

TESSA

Mrs. Butcher. A bed wetter if ever I seen one!

CASS

(*impetuously*): Hi, kid.

TRILBE

I would hazard a guess that our friend is not of a jovial disposition.

CASS

You kinda liked these, I think. Catch. Go on. Take it. It ain't rat poison.

TESSA

It's not the flowers, is it?

CASS

Take them away before I get mean again. And a happy Christmas to you.

TESSA

And the same to you, Miss McGuire. And thanks very much. No matter what the matron says, I knew you were a lady.

Exits

CASS

Well, you can tell the matron from me that if she was on fire I wouldn't—Agh! Now what did I do that for!

TRILBE

She's engaged, you know.

CASS

Matron?!

TRILBE

Tessa. She's going to be married in the spring.

CASS

Yeah? . . . In the spring? . . .

INGRAM

They're an excellent match for my new suit.

TRILBE

The Christmas atmosphere is really building up.

CASS *has nothing for* TRILBE *now except the gloves.*

CASS

(*busily*): Yeah, and I got something for you, too, Trilbe, like I said . . . you bet . . . and I give it some thought . . . and finally I came to the conclusion that what you needed most—

TRILBE

An accessory.

CASS

A pair of warm gloves—that's what it is—cos this place, hell, it would freeze the hair off a bald man. So that's what I went and got you—a pair of woollen gloves— mebbe a bit on the big side but they'll shrink, won't they? Warm—woollen gloves—and a happy Christmas to you.

TRILBE

Like Mr. Ingram, Catherine, I'm speechless, I really am.

CASS

That's a change.

TRILBE

I'm deeply grateful to you. Thank you.

CASS

Forget it.

An awkwardness descends. The brief elation dies.

CASS

(*continued*): And that's about it. Everything's gone. All my worldly goods. (*Looking into bag*) Nothing left.

CASS *returns to the mantelpiece. The silence flows in. To stop it:*

INGRAM

Mr. Quinn was a . . . a . . . he was a lighthearted man.

TRILBE

He has gone, Mr. Ingram.

INGRAM

I know. I know.

TRILBE

To a nephew who owns a substantial farm.

INGRAM

He told me.

TRILBE

He never really belonged, you know.

INGRAM

In a way.

TRILBE

Oh, no; he was never fully one of us.

INGRAM

I suppose not.

TRILBE

A willing little man, I'll grant you, but never one of us. Don't you agree, Catherine?

CASS *moves away from the mantelpiece. She is looking at one of the cards. For the first time she is vague, dreamy, remote. And when she speaks, all brashness is gone from her voice.*

CASS

One Christmas I saw a man in a green sledge in Central Park, and he was being pulled along by two beautiful chestnuts. He must ov been a very rich man to keep two chestnuts in Manhattan, I'll tell you. And the horses they had these bells on their harness, you know, like music . . .

She goes towards the winged chair and stands beside it.

CASS

(*continued*): And as he was passing me he happened to look over. And do you know what he done? He lifted his black hat to me . . .

TRILBE

(*softly*): Tell us, Catherine.

CASS

There's nothing to tell, really . . . just a man with a kind face and two chestnuts and a green sledge and the white of the snow and the music of the bells . . . and he looked at me and he lifted his black hat to me, that gentleman in Central Park did . . .

TRILBE

Tell us.

INGRAM

Tell us.

TRILBE

Tell us.

CASS *suddenly bursts into tears and drops into the winged chair. There she cries and groans, covering her face with her hands while the spasm lasts. Then, emerging from it, she sits up straight, almost with nobility, and very slowly lets her head come to rest on the back of the chair.*

TRILBE

Perhaps you should read to us, Mr. Ingram.

INGRAM

I never get a chance to finish.

TRILBE

Tell us the end of one of your stories, then.

INGRAM

I'll finish the Tristan story. I know it by heart.

Fade in slowly and with growing volume the Liebestod from "Tristan und Isolde."

After a few seconds of the music, CASS *begins to speak. She becomes more and more assured, as if the recounting of the events made their memory and their accuracy more vivid.*

CASS

I stood at the stern of the ship, and two white and green lines spread out and out and out before me. And the gentleman I worked for, Mr. Olsen, he was only a few years older than me, tall and straight and manly, with golden hair and kind soft patient eyes. And I had two dimples ... (*Very rapidly: suddenly agitated*) What—what—where—what am I—?

TRILBE

No, no, go on, go on. Golden hair and patient eyes. And you had two dimples ...

CASS

(*relaxing*): Yeah—yeah—two dimples ... And he would make me laugh and put his fingers into the dimples and say, "Hooked you, baby." And the morning we got married my father he stood up and sung "Oft in the Stilly Night 'Ere Slumber's Chains Have Bound Me," and people there said if he had ov been a younger man he would ov made the big time, he was that good, my father; and Mr. Joseph Bolowski he played classical tunes on the piano; and Mr. Slinger he was the toastmaster; and everyone was so gay, so gay ...

INGRAM

But even though they were separated by exile, Tristan's love for Isolde grew; and finally he sent for her.

CASS

And we moved into this great big ten-roomed apartment on the West Side, and from our bedroom window we could see the ships sailing off to South America and the Bahamas . . . and Ireland . . . and Glasgow . . . And all round the walls were pictures of Harry's kids; I was their Auntie Cass, you see; and regular as the clock came their letters—I have them all—fine kids . . .

TRILBE

A doctor, a priest, an architect, a student.

CASS

And when I came back home they were all down at Cork to meet me; and Harry and Alice and Momma; and Connie he wanted us to stay over with his folks in Dublin, but Harry wouldn't hear of that; and all the cars drove up, one behind the other, like it was a parade or something, some of them with chauffeurs and all, right up Harry's big wide avenue, underneath all them golden chestnuts, and all our friends came in and we had such a party . . .

INGRAM

And at his bidding she came to him on a ship. But he, wounded on his couch, was too weak to meet her. And she got off the ship and rushed to his side and embraced him. And he died in her arms.

CASS

And Connie and me we slipped out by the back and went for a walk out to the crooked bridge and he said to me, "Do you remember, Cass? Do you remember?"—as if I ever forgot, even for a second. And we must ov spent so long out there that Harry he got worried and went searching for us, and the police they were searching, too. And when we got back the party was over, and the house was quiet, and Momma she and I had a long chat together, private, confidential, my momma and me. And then I told Harry that I was going to move out cos I wanted to be independent; but he wouldn't listen to me, not Harry, he's too stubborn. But I insisted. So we bought this place close to the sea and we fixed it up and Harry's kids they come to see us all the time and play around on the beach; and we work and work and don't have no time to think . . .

INGRAM

And she died, too, of love. And from their grave two rose trees grew up and intertwined so that they could never be separated again.

CASS

Connie and Father and Harry and Jeff and the four kids and Joe and Slinger . . . and I love them all so much, and they love me so much; we're so lucky, so lucky in our love. (*To* TRILBE) What is it you say?

TRILBE

But I being poor—

CASS

—have only my dreams. I have spread my dreams under your feet.

INGRAM

Tread softly—

CASS

—because you tread on my dreams.

TRILBE

Our truth.

INGRAM

Our truth.

CASS

Our truth.

The music fades. Enter MRS. BUTCHER.

BUTCHER

(*too loudly*): Good evening to you.

She goes immediately down front and sits on an upright chair, her back resolutely to the others. She opens a magazine and pretends she is reading. She addresses the audience confidentially.

BUTCHER

My God, would you just look at them! If you met them on a dark night, you would think you were doting.

The gong goes.

TRILBE

Ah! Teatime! And how are you, m'dear?

BUTCHER *realizes she is being addressed.*

BUTCHER

What—what's that?

TRILBE

You're well, I trust.

BUTCHER

Nothing wrong with me. Thanks be to God I was never a burden to anybody.

INGRAM *and* **TRILBE** *get their things together to go off for tea.*

TRILBE

(*to* **BUTCHER**): We're having cold ham for tea this evening. Sometimes rather tasty. And General Custer tomorrow night.

BUTCHER

(*direct to audience*): Our Lady of the Seven Snows!

TRILBE

A film of the Ninety-eight Rebellion.

BUTCHER

(*to audience*): Lunatics is sane compared with these ones!

INGRAM

(*to* TRILBE): Would the lady . . . is she . . . d'you think she would care to . . . to . . . to . . . to join us?

TRILBE

(*to* BUTCHER): The dining room's along here, m'dear.

BUTCHER

Carry on. I can look after myself.

INGRAM

(*to* TRILBE): Perhaps I should . . . should I . . . ?

TRILBE

Much too soon. She's still at *that* stage. Catherine?

CASS

Yeah—yeah—coming—sure.

TRILBE

(*to* INGRAM): I do believe I'm getting the Christmas spirit fully now. (*Sings*) "*Good King Wenceslas looked out . . .*"

INGRAM *joins her and they exit singing.* CASS *sees* BUTCHER *sitting alone and crosses to her.*

CASS

You gotta eat, you know. You can't go without your vittles.

BUTCHER

I can look after myself, thank you very much. (*To audience*) Has she a drink on her?

CASS

My name's Olsen, by the way. My late husband—mebbe you heard of him—General Cornelius Olsen—he made quite a name for himself in the last war. But you just call me Catherine.

BUTCHER

(*to audience*): Full!

CASS

I dunno, but I think it's better to get into the routine here right away. (*Coaxing*) You'll like the tea they make. It looks like horse's—it looks like it was treacle, but it sure has a kick.

BUTCHER

You just run along now and have your meal.

CASS *hesitates. She is conscious that she has some intelligence she could communicate, if only she knew what that intelligence was.*

CASS

When I first came here—

TESSA *appears at the door.*

TESSA

(*to* BUTCHER): You! You're wanted in the matron's office to sign some forms.

BUTCHER

If you're addressing me, my name happens to be Mrs. Elizabeth Butcher, and I'm accustomed to—

TESSA

And she says be quick about it.

BUTCHER

(*direct to audience*): Maybe I should keep on the right side of that matron one. Not that I'll be here for long.

(*Rises to leave*) Stay where you are. I'll be back in a minute.

She goes off right with pathetic dignity.

TESSA
You! You're going the wrong way. Matron's office is back.

BUTCHER *leaves.*

CASS
She'll learn, sweetie. She'll learn.

TESSA
Huh! And the airs of her! You'd think she *was* somebody!

Suddenly coy: drawing CASS's *attention to the artificial flowers she was given, as a preliminary to showing off her ring.*

TESSA
Nice?

CASS
Elegant.

TESSA
And what about that?

CASS
What?

TESSA

Engaged.

CASS

Well, well, well!

TESSA

(*by rote*): It's a solitaire diamond surrounded by a cluster of dazzling rubies and mounted on plat-ig-num and gold.

CASS *catches her hand and searches earnestly.*

CASS

Where's the diamond?

TESSA

God, are you blind, too! There!

CASS

Oh yeah—yeah—so it is. Gee, that's nice, sweetie.

TESSA *moves away, lost in contemplation of her ring.*

CASS

(*continues*): Would you do me a favor?

TESSA

(*not listening*): What?

CASS

I got this only brother, see, Harry, and I expect he'll drop in to see me some time this evening, you know, for Christmas and all; and I want you to tell me as soon as he comes, sweetie, cos I don't want that matron to turn him away or nuthin'. That would hurt him. And make a big fuss about him, honey, will you. All his days he's been kicked around. Treat him like he was important, you know.

TESSA

He old, too?

CASS

Harry? No, Harry's not old. But he's one of those guys— you know—he never got nuthin' much outa life. Just the two of us, and I guess he didn't have it good. I was the one that made it.

TESSA

We're going to spend our honeymoon in Glasgow.

CASS

You'll keep an eye out for him, sweetie?

TESSA

Alright. (*Leaving*) Come on. Your tea's ready.

CASS

(*to herself*): Poor, poor Harry . . . (*She sighs at* HARRY's *bad luck. Then brightens, looks around the common room with calm satisfaction*) Home at last. Gee, but it's a good thing to be home.

She lifts her bags that she always carries, takes another contented look around, and goes off singing her own version of "Good King Wenceslas."

CURTAIN

The first performance of *The Loves of Cass McGuire* was presented at the Helen Hayes Theatre, New York, on October 6, 1966, by the David Merrick Arts Foundation. It was directed by Hilton Edwards, and the setting was by Lloyd Burlingame. The cast was as follows:

Mother: FRANCES BRANDT

Dom: DON SCARDINO

Alice: SYLVIA O'BRIEN

Harry: LIAM REDMOND

Cass: RUTH GORDON

Tessa: MARY GREANEY

Pat Quinn: ARTHUR O'SULLIVAN

Trilbe Costello: BRENDA FORBES

Mr. Ingram: DENNIS KING

Mrs. Butcher: DOROTHY BLACKBURN